CHOOSE HAPPY

CHOOSE HAPPY

MELODY ROSS

BRAVEGIRLS Club

Andrews McMeel
Publishing

Kansas City • Sydney • London

Dear Beloved Soul,

I want to talk about having a happy life.

You have already been through so much. You know that sometimes happiness is easy to come by, and sometimes happiness is very hard to find. The truth is, it takes a lot of discipline to choose happy. The beauty of life is that we get to try again every single day.

Every morning is a fresh start to ask yourself... "What if something absolutely wonderful happens today?"

The most important lesson we can learn is that
we can still choose happy even when it doesn't
feel as though happy is choosing us. That's where
the discipline comes in. That's what makes your
happiness a gift to everyone who knows you.

We are all here to be happy. The more of us
choose joy and happiness, the better the world
will be. Because you know what? A bunch of happy
people makes for a really happy world.

xoxo,
Melody

Stay in your own Life

We all have a different

journey, a different path.

Don't compare your path with

that of others, dear soul.

Comparing never does any good.

Your path

is *your path*

. . .the very path

you

were created

to travel.

Stay in

your own

perfect life.

Look for
What is Right

When you feel stuck in situations or relationships that feel all wrong, look for what is right. When you are faced with a difficult human being, one of the most beautiful and light-filled things you can do is to go to the ends of the earth to look for what is beautiful and true and right about that person.

There are *gifts* to be found

in everything,

even if those gifts

are simply the lessons

we learn from difficult

situations and people.

We find

miracles

when we look for

what is right.

Do it for Yourself

We must all remember that

no one else is going to

make our dreams come true for us.

It is your job to get

up every day and work toward

the things that

are deepest in your heart...

Just as it is

the job

of every

last one of us.

So do *your* job.
Do it for
yourself.

Start today
No More
Excuses

We put things off. It's easier to do anything else than the yucky stuff and the hard stuff and the mind bending stuff. But the flipped-on-its-head fact is that when we do the hardest things first, *We feel better*. Waaaay better. And those yucky things that seemed so big and burdensome turn out to be not so big after all.

Let's do the hardest things first

and see how much better we feel

for the rest of the day.

How much lighter . . .

Start today.

Let it Go

We hold on to so much stuff
that weighs us down—
grudges, regrets,
outdated dreams,
crummy beliefs about ourselves,
even ratty old clothes—
all things that
make us feel bad...
but that we hold onto.

*Wouldn't today be a great day
to let some of it go?*

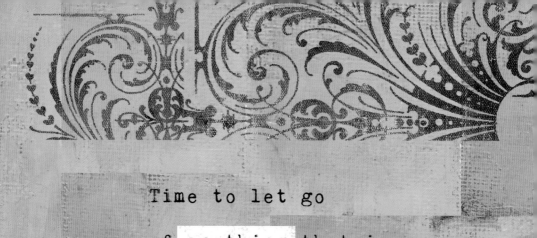

Time to let go

of **anything** that is

weighing you down,

beautiful soul...

You'll fly better.

Sometimes we don't know what to do...or we
are just too tired to know what to do.
Sometimes we hide and wait because we don't
feel like we are quite ready yet, or the
circumstances quite right yet...or sometimes
maybe we are afraid.
THESE ARE THE VERY MOST IMPORTANT TIMES
to show up to your life...and keep showing up.

This

is

when

the

magic

happens...

When you just *show up.*

Life sometimes leaves us in limbo, without the answers we want or without any answers at all. We suffer and suffer when we imagine the things that MIGHT happen to us.

Peace will come

when we remember that whatever

happens, we will get through.

We may not be sure

what's ahead,

but we can be sure

we will be okay.

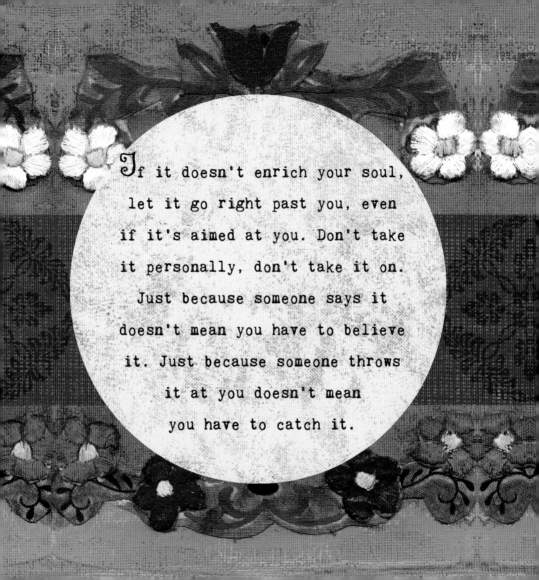

If it doesn't enrich your soul,
let it go right past you, even
if it's aimed at you. Don't take
it personally, don't take it on.
Just because someone says it
doesn't mean you have to believe
it. Just because someone throws
it at you doesn't mean
you have to catch it.

$\mathcal{L}$et others own their own words, their own actions, and their own reactions. And let us use the beautiful gift of choice to take responsibility for our own.

$\mathcal{D}$on't
put out a
catcher's mitt.
Step aside,
beautiful friend,
and let it go
right past you.

Cheer
for
Yourself

Sometimes you are the only person alive who knows what you are truly trying to do in the world, what you are struggling for and working toward. . . . So you are the only person who knows when you have gotten there.

That means you have got
to be your own biggest cheerleader.

This does not make your victory

any less important.

In fact, the victories that only

you know about

are very often the most important

victories of all.

So be good to yourself.

Praise yourself

You know best how very much

you deserve it.

Are you working hard to

make things make sense,

exhausting yourself

with battling?

Set yourself free.

Go with the sweet flow

instead of

struggling against it.

Surrender

to how things are.

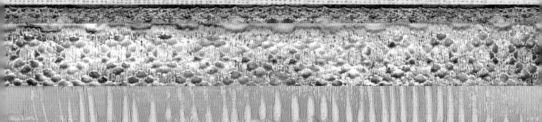

Remember, you have *your own kind* of
wings. Find them and use them.

I wish we didn't forget
so often how important
it is to do this.
We are so mean to ourselves.
Kindness matters so much...

Just one little

act of kindness makes

so much difference....So

turn things around

with kindness...

Beginning with

Yourself.

Keep
Going
Anyway

We have all overcome something.

We all face things that are

difficult, tedious, thankless,

exhausting, scary. That's all

part of the journey.

Keep trying, keep fighting, keep working at it, keep your head up, *keep praying,* keep caring, keep on keeping on . . .

Stay strong
and
keep going.

Be True
to
Yourself

When we are **very true** to who we are, not everyone likes it. It can be hard.

It can be uncomfortable.

But **being who you are** is good for you. And it is *good for everyone else, too.*

Be willing to do

the stuff

not everyone

likes.

You'll find

it feels

good

to stay true

to yourself.

Stay
Happy

whenever you get

the chance to be happy

Life is tough. It's just flat-out hard, and mean, and cruel. You deserve a beautiful day in the sunshine with a big grin on your face once in a while. So don't let anybody steal happiness away from you—*including yourself*.

There's enough

happiness

to go around.

It's not going to run out.

And it's contagious.

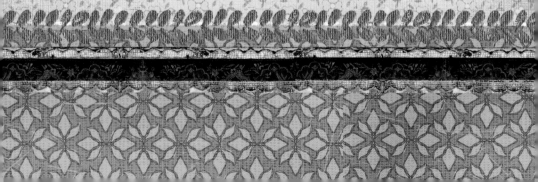

When you have a

smooth stretch

in the road,

it's a gift.

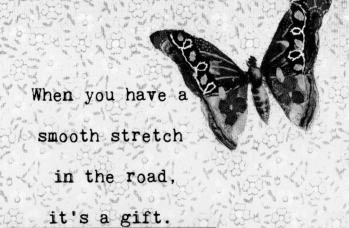

Enjoy it!

Let Yourself
Be
Awesome

Let's be brave enough

to dream big, huge,

embarrassingly impossible

dreams.

What are you waiting for?

No more hiding out

and holding back.

Let awesomeness in.

And let yourself

be everything

you dream of.

It's Not Too Late

not ever, to grow up

To Be the Person

you wanted to

Grow Up to Be

When you were a little girl, what were your hopes and ambitions that were unique and wonderful and unabashed? And what held you back, as you grew older, from wanting or working for those *tender dreams?*

Don't be afraid to be

that amazing woman

you saw in your future

when you were young.

Uncover those dreams again.

Honor the person

you were born to be.

Love her. Protect her.

And never let anyone

talk you out of

BEING *her.*

Honor the
Seasons
of Your Life

Some seasons are easy and breezy, some very difficult. Some are filled with people and support; others we have to travel alone. Some seasons make perfect sense; some seem to make no sense at all.

Some seasons change everything, and nothing is the same again.

Please don't forget that there is a plan for your life. Each season always shows up when it is supposed to, always lasts as long as it's supposed to last, and always teaches us exactly what we need to learn. *Life is incredible like that.*

Find the *beauty* in every season, and learn the lessons of each.

All OF OUR SEASONS MAKE US WHO WE ARE.

Everything You Need

You Already Have

The truth is that you have everything it takes to do the *beautiful and extraordinary* things that only you can do. We are completely capable of doing the things that our hearts yearn to do, to give the things that are within us to give, to heal our heart-hurts, to live the lovely lives our souls cry out to live.

And so we
simply must
go out and
be extraordinary...

for we have

everything

we need.

Melody Ross is a world-renowned artist, author, and entrepreneur. In her twenties she built one of the most collected and sought-after brands in the designer paper industry, and has gone on to design licensed products for leading scrapbooking, home decor, giftwares, and textile companies. Melody and her story and products have appeared in many magazines, books, and TV programs, and she has been the recipient of awards from the Alfred P. Sloan Foundation, the National Association of Women Business Owners, and the Craft & Hobby Association.

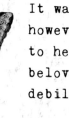

It was a very personal trauma, however, that put her on the path to her true life's work. In 2004 her beloved husband, Marq, sustained a debilitating brain injury.

During the years Melody devoted herself to his recovery, they lost nearly everything, including the successful company they had built together—but they managed to keep their marriage and family intact.

In 2009, Melody started Brave Girls Club with her sister Kathy; every day since has been a beautiful, wild adventure of doing everything she loves most with the people she loves most. Melody hosts Brave Girl Camp art retreats and workshops at her ranch in Idaho as well as hugely popular online art courses subscribed to by students from around the world, where she teaches everything she knows about art and the healing power of happiness and unconditional love.

Andrews McMeel Publishing, LLC
an Andrews McMeel Universal company
1130 Walnut Street, Kansas City, Missouri 64106

www.andrewsmcmeel.com

15 16 17 18 19 TEN 10 9 8 7 6 5 4 3 2 1

ISBN: 978-1-4494-6724-1

Library of Congress Control Number: 2014954106

ATTENTION: SCHOOLS AND BUSINESSES

Andrews McMeel books are available at quantity discounts with
bulk purchase for educational, business, or sales promotional
use. For information, please e-mail the Andrews McMeel
Publishing Special Sales Department:
specialsales@amuniversal.com.